Cranbury Public Library

D1541206

WHOSE TEETH ARE THESE?

JOANNE RANDOLPH

PowerKiDS
press.
New York

Published in 2009 by The Rosen Publishing Group, Inc.
29 East 21st Street, New York, NY 10010

First Edition

Book Design: Julio Gil
Photo Researcher: Jessica Gerweck

Photo Credits: Cover, pp. 5, 7 © Biosphoto/Allofs Thoe/Peter Arnold; pp. 9, 11, 13, 15, 17, 19, 23, 24 Shutterstock.com; p. 21 © age fotostock/SuperStock.

Library of Congress Cataloging-in-Publication Data

Randolph, Joanne.
  Whose teeth are these? / Joanne Randolph. — 1st ed.
      p. cm. — (Animal clues)
  Includes index.
  ISBN 978-1-4042-4456-6 (library binding)
  1. Teeth—Juvenile literature. I. Title.
  QL858.R35 2009
  590—dc22
                                                2007048205

Manufactured in the United States of America

CONTENTS

Which orange and black cat has huge, sharp teeth?

An orange and black tiger has huge, sharp teeth.

Whose **cone**-shaped teeth snap together to catch dinner?

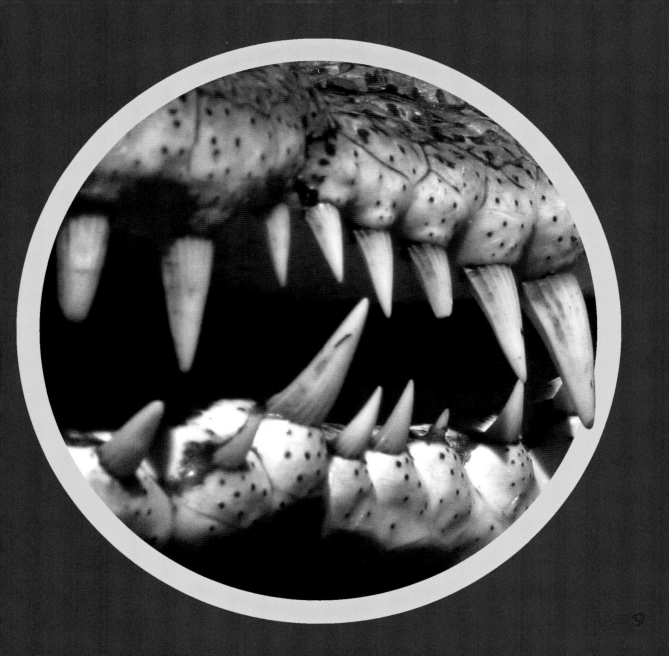

This crocodile's cone-shaped teeth snap together to catch dinner.

To whom do these skin-covered teeth called **fangs** belong?

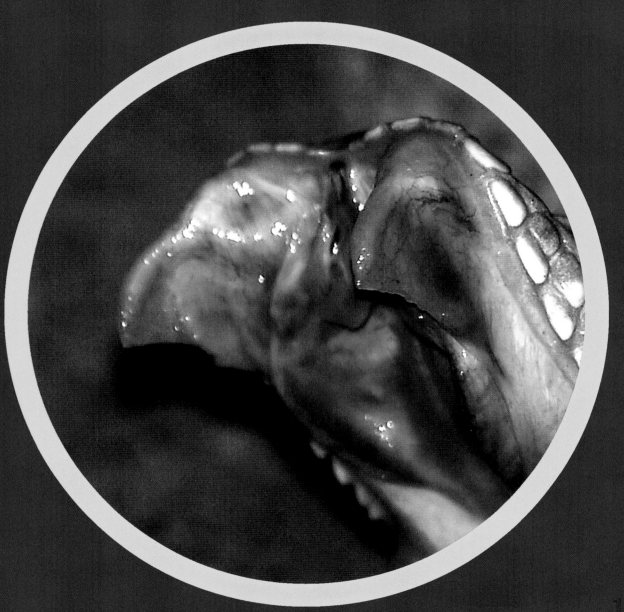

These skin-covered fangs belong to a rattlesnake.

Which fish belongs to these teeth shaped like **triangles**?

A piranha belongs to these teeth shaped like triangles.

Which furry, brown animal has teeth that never stop growing?

This furry, brown groundhog has teeth that never stop growing.

WORDS TO KNOW

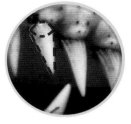

cone

fangs

triangles

INDEX

WEB SITES

Due to the changing nature of Internet links, PowerKids Press has developed an online list of Web sites related to the subject of this book. This site is updated regularly. Please use this link to access the list:
www.powerkidslinks.com/acl/teeth/